The Smart & Easy Guide To Home Buying: How to Buy Your First Home & Get Your Mortgage Home Financing in Place Successfully

Mark Dennison

Legal Stuff

COPYRIGHT

Copyright © 2013 Checkmate Marketing Group LLC. All rights reserved worldwide.

No part of this publication may be replicated, redistributed, or given away in any form without the prior written consent of the author and publisher.

Checkmate Marketing Group LLC

LIMITATION OF LIABILITY

THE MATERIALS IN THIS BOOK ARE PROVIDED "AS IS" WITHOUT ANY EXPRESS OR IMPLIED WARRANTY OF ANY KIND INCLUDING WARRANTIES OF MERCHANTABILITY, NONINFRINGEMENT OF INTELLECTUAL PROPERTY, OR FITNESS FOR ANY PARTICULAR PURPOSE. IN NO EVENT SHALL OR ITS AGENTS OR OFFICERS BE LIABLE FOR ANY DAMAGES WHATSOEVER (INCLUDING, WITHOUT LIMITATION, DAMAGES FOR LOSS OF PROFITS, BUSINESS INTERRUPTION, LOSS OF INFORMATION, INJURY OR DEATH) ARISING OUT OF THE USE OF OR INABILITY TO USE THE MATERIALS, EVEN IF HAS BEEN ADVISED OF THE POSSIBILITY OF SUCH LOSS OR DAMAGES.

Table of Contents

Renting Vs. Owning: How to Make the Leap 4
How to Enjoy Home Buying 8
Making Your First Property Purchase 11
Tips for First Time Buyers: Things to Know Before You Sign .. 14
Knowing Your Real Estate: How to Find and Evaluate Potential Properties 17
Make Sure You Can Afford the House You Want 19
How to Hire a Good Real Estate Agent 24
Hanging on to Your Money 26
How to Spot a Scam Before It Spots You 29
Creative Ways to Finance Your Home 33
FICO: Your Credit Score and You 36
Loan Pre-Approval and What It Means 39
Understanding Loan Options 42
Finding the Perfect Mortgage 46
Insurance and Risk Management: Everything You Need to Know 52
Save Money With an Inspection 55
Preparing to Buy a Home 58
We Want Your Feedback on This Book! 59

Renting Vs. Owning: How to Make the Leap

Everyone reaches a stage in their life where they feel ready to quit renting and purchase their own home. Especially for those who are beginning a family, buying a home may seem like the ultimate strong beginning. Owning your own home provides a sense of emotional and financial security, and also offers a foundation for a sense of community connection and involvement. If owning your own home is one of your long term goals, it may seem like the obvious choice. However, choosing to buy a home is a huge decision. There are several benefits to both renting a home and owning a home. To help you decide which option is right for you, let's have a look at the advantages and disadvantages of buying your first home.

Advantages:

- You Are Your Own Landlord

- Provides a Sense of Security

- Great Investment for the Future

- Greater Freedom

- You Qualify for Tax Rebates and/or Deductions

- Cheaper than Renting Long Term

- Every Payment is an Investment

- No Limitations on Decorating or Renovating

- Builds Equity Over Time

- Improves Credit for Future Loans

Disadvantages

- Liability for Accidents and Injuries on Your Property

- Liability to Neighboring Property Damage if Caused by Your Property

- You Are Responsible for Maintenance and Upkeep

- Your New Home Is Your Long Term Living Arrangement

- Loan Debt Is Present Until Paid Off

- You Must Provide Your Own Insurance

- Equity Rates Can Change

- Large Down Payment is Required

- Property Taxes Can Be Expensive

Most people start out renting an apartment or house. While most people hope to own their own home eventually, some are comfortable with renting for their entire life. Renting is a good option that comes with several freedoms that are not present when buying a home, but there are disadvantages as well. Let's examine the advantages and disadvantages of renting.

Advantages:

- Freedom to Move Once Your Lease is Up

- Freedom to Downsize if Your Financial Situation Changes

- Maintenance is Not Your Responsibility

- Rent Often Includes Utilities

- Free Use of Public Amenities May be Available

Disadvantages:

- Little to No Freedom to Remodel, Paint or Decorate

- Rent is Subject to Increase

- You Get Limited Space for a High Price

- You Do Not Qualify for Tax Deductions

- You Can Be Evicted With Little Notice

- You May Have Restrictions on Pets, Noise, and Lifestyle

- Limits on Family Size are Often Present

- Your Rent is Not an Investment

As you can see, there are advantages and disadvantages both to renting and to owning. Either has the potential of being a comfortable and satisfying way to live. Thus, the decision of whether to rent or own your home should fit your emotional, financial, and lifestyle needs. When deciding whether or not to buy a home, it is also important to consider your future. Where will you be financially in ten years? In the future, will you want the freedom to move as desired, or will you be comfortable being tied down to one property?

Choosing to buy a home is a huge decision and not one to be taken lightly. Give yourself the time you need to think about your options.

How to Enjoy Home Buying

Home buying is often nerve-wracking and stressful. This is especially true for inexperienced first time home buyers. It is understandable that such a life altering experience would be stressful rather than enjoyable. Buying a home is a decision that can last a lifetime, and, in many cases, your investment may become a generational tradition. All of these facts make it easy to see why fun and home buying are generally completely unrelated.

Buyers, especially first time buyers, are often intimidated by the large number of factors included in the purchase of a home. In particular, many prospective buyers stress over the legal aspects of buying a home. The financial aspect is another major stressor. Additional stressful factors include dealing with brokers, agents, and insurance companies. And, if your first home buying experience does not go exactly as planned, which it often the case, that can be particularly stressful as well.

Fortunately, buying your first home does not have to be intimidating or incredibly stressful. By adding some diversity to your property choices and examining each road block along the way, it is possible to make home buying less intimidating and ultimately more enjoyable.

Next, we will discuss the five steps to purchasing your new home successfully. Let's take a look at the challenges and solutions that apply to each stage of the purchasing process.

Step 1: Understanding Your Finances

Understanding your financial situation can be difficult. Can you afford to buy your own home, make a large down payment, and continue making long term mortgage payments? Speaking with a financial advisor can make these questions much less intimidating. A financial advisor will help you employ a strategy to pay for your home over time. A financial advisor is also helpful if you have a questionable credit history, other debts, or financial hardships. Ultimately, a financial advisor will help you find a happy medium between your dream home and your price range.

Step 2: Select Potential Properties

There are many real estate options available on the market today, even for first time home buyers. The variety of methods through which you can find a suitable property is exciting! Every potential buyer should take full advantage of the survey methods that modern technology makes available to them. Rather than just driving around your desired neighborhood seeking For Sale signs, hunt for houses you like in newspapers, real estate magazines, brochures, advertisements, and online. Friends and family are also a great source of property recommendations.

Step 3: Seek Advice

Even as a first time property buyer, you do not have to make the mistakes that many first timers make. By seeking advice from people who have learned hard lessons during the home buying process, it is completely possible to avoid making the same mistakes yourself. Whether you are a veteran home buyer or a first time buyer, learning from others' mistakes is a great way to avoid unnecessary headache related to purchasing real estate.

Step 4: Secure a Great Agent

It is easy to underestimate the value of an agent. However, finding an agent is perhaps the most important step in the home buying process, second only to selecting a property. Many prospective buyers do not actually select their agent, but find one more or less by accident. It is wise to instead choose an agent whose skills fit your personal home buying needs. An effective real estate agent is crucial to the success of your home buying journey and can save you quite a bit of headache.

Step 5: Close the Deal

Closing a deal on a house is a process in and of itself. Closing the deal involves a great deal of steps, including a lot of paperwork and discussions. Even though closing the deal can be difficult, it is usually one of the most exciting stages of the home buying process. This stage is where the buyer and the seller make an agreement on the financial aspect of the sale, complete paperwork, and address any important details. Finally, the seller hand over the keys and the buyer is welcome into their new home.

Making Your First Property Purchase

Buying your first home is exciting and risky; exciting because it is risky and risky because it is exciting. It is easy to look at rising real estate prices and see how profitable it would be to pick a house up cheap, flip it, and sell it at a high cost. However, it is important that you also look at the risks of home buying. There are ways to keep the excitement of home buying, but also minimize the risks and increase your profit. Let's take a look at some smart property buying strategies.

1. Do Your Research:

Buying your first property can be exciting, but it is best to look at your decision from a practical standpoint. Research the local real estate market, and be realistic when examining your own lifestyle and financial situation. Buying a home you do not want and cannot sell can leave you with a lifelong burden.

Talk to local real estate agents, or go online and do some research to get an idea of property prices in your desired area. This will give you a good idea of whether or not you need to broaden your search.

Gathering information on the legal side of real estate purchase is also a good idea. Learn what you can about any legal restrictions or requirements that may be present. Learn about contracts, escrow, titles, homeowner's insurance, and the typical closing procedures in your area. It is also a good idea to be aware of the role each individual professional plays in the property buying process. Remember that every professional has their own fees, and it is a good idea to shop around for the lowest price. The more information you gather, the more prepared you will be to purchase your first property.

2. Get Financed:

Ready to take the plunge? Before you even begin looking at properties, you should get financing lined up. There are a variety of ways to go about financing. To save yourself the most money in the long run, you should talk to quite a few individuals and organizations. Talk with lenders such as banks, mortgage companies, and internet home loan lenders. Then discuss your budget and answer any questions each lender has. You will want your credit score as high as possible, and should try to remove any negative credit reports from your credit score. If possible, this should be done before you begin the buying process, since lenders will thoroughly examine your credit score before qualifying you for a loan.

Be sure to ask each potential lender about available financing plans and options. There are many options for financing your real estate purchase and they vary in their rates, down payments, and financial consequences. Any time you take out a loan, you are taking on a large financial responsibility, and you should be prepared for the liabilities that are involved.

3. Find a Property

Perhaps the most exciting, and potentially the most stressful, part of the home buying process is finding a home you want to spend your life in. Try to find a property that is profitable. Do not look just at the property, but also at the neighborhood. Whether your house is a castle or a fixer upper, the property value will deteriorate if the neighborhood is less than desirable.

Start by finding a desirable location, and then look for real estate in that location. While it is a good idea to look in newspapers, ads, and online, you will also want to drive around the neighborhood and look for "For Sale By Owner" signs posted on properties. Abandoned properties are not necessarily a bad idea, either, if you are interested in making renovations. This can be a cost effective way to secure your dream home.

Is your financing secure? Great! Once you have found the perfect property, be it move-in ready or a diamond in the rough, it is time to talk to your agent and put in an offer. Keep in mind that you want the lowest price possible, while the seller will try to get the highest price possible. Do not be afraid to negotiate, but do not expect to get a great property for nothing.

It is always a good idea to compromise with the seller. If you want repairs made before you move in, expect to compromise with the seller on move in dates and other small details. Both parties can leave satisfied, or both parties can leave bitter with no sale made. Be firm, but remember that compromise is important as well.

Most importantly, enjoy your first home buying experience! It is a real adventure!

Tips for First Time Buyers: Things to Know Before You Sign

You have decided you are ready to buy a home, and you have enough money in savings to make the initial down payment on a property. Buying a home is an experience that is stressful for everyone. However, first time home owners have the added pressure of the unknown which can make buying a home additionally stressful. Let's go over some tips to make the whole process easier and less stressful for first time buyers.

1. Understand Your Finances

Make sure you have enough money to buy a home. While home loans will provide much of your budget, you will also be expected to come up with a large down payment on your own. Make sure you have enough money to cover this expense. Also, keep an eye on your credit history; make sure that any debts or bad credit reports are cleared up as quickly as possible. This will make the buying process go much smoother for you. You should also understand what your financial situation looks like, so that you can limit your house hunting to properties that are within your budget. Understanding your budget and sticking to it will save you a lot of heartache later when you fall in love with a house that is not within your price range.

2. Know What You Want

Before you start house hunting, you need to have an idea of what you are looking for. It is important to have a good idea of what kind of house and area you want to live in. Think about features that are important to you. Do you want an oversized bath? A fenced in yard? A home within walking distance of shopping districts? Keep these details in mind when you begin shopping for a house. It is a smart idea to prepare a list of questions that you can refer back to for each property you look at. This will help you make a final decision on a property. Include questions that are important to you in a home. Some questions to ask yourself include:

- Is the house in a good neighborhood?

- Is the house the right size for your present and future needs?

- How long is the commute to your workplace?

- Is there access to public transportation?

- Does the house need repairs? What will they cost?

- How is the resale value?

3. Do Your Research

If you think research is a repetitive theme, you are correct! Doing your research is crucial to the entire buying process. It is important to research the types of mortgages and mortgage terms that you are eligible for. This will give you a better idea of your financial standing after you make your purchase. Also, be sure to read up on your real estate agent. Finding an agent who is knowledgeable in the local housing market and able to answer all of your questions will ensure that the entire process goes smoothly for you. Make sure that your agent has your best interests in mind, rather than their own interests or even the seller's interests. Try to build a strong professional relationship with your real estate agent immediately. This can help make the buying process easier.

4. Trust Your Instincts

The majority of first time buyers have buyer's remorse sometime after moving into their new home. They wonder if they can really afford their home, if they made the right decision, or if a better house might have come on the market eventually. If and when this happens, try to remember what made you fall in love with your new house in the first place. Trust your instincts. You bought this house for a reason!

Knowing Your Real Estate: How to Find and Evaluate Potential Properties

Investing in real estate is undoubtedly easier than it has ever been before. However, even in a great housing market, it is easy to drop a lot of money on a not-so-great house. Let's take a look at some tips that can help you maximize your investment.

1. Use the Internet

The internet is a fantastic resource for potential real estate buyers. Thanks to a variety of websites and open forum listings, you can spend countless hours searching for houses. It is also possible to find out a good deal of information on these potential properties, including price, pictures, and legal information. To minimize realtor fees, you can search for "For Sale By Owner" listings. Also take a look at real estate websites, but be expected to pay additional fees.

2. Do Some Leg Work

It is not a great idea to find a house through the internet or print listings alone. A smart buyer does some leg work, because they know that seeing a house in person is necessary in order to be certain you are getting what you think you are. Check out the house. See how it feels as you take a walkthrough. Could you live there? Be sure to check out the surrounding neighborhood for signs of decrepit properties which could lower your property value. While you are driving to and from selected properties, keep an eye out for "For Sale By Owner" signs, as well as realtor signs.

Before you make an offer on a home, be sure to make multiple visits. If possible, make visits at different times of the day and in varying weather. A house that is beautiful in warm weather could flood when it rains. Try to keep an eye on these details in order to minimize your repair cost and maximize your property satisfaction.

3. Get an Inspection

If you find a house you love, get a contingent deal in place. For real estate purposes, a contingent deal is one that is dependent upon a satisfactory property inspection. Once you have examined the property yourself and found it satisfactory, you will need to hire a professional home inspector to evaluate the property as well. It is also beneficial to know enough about property inspection to keep the inspector honest. Of course, most inspectors are already honest so this is not crucial, but still recommended.

Keep in mind that not everything will be 100% perfect when you plan to purchase your new home. Review the inspector's report carefully. Major and minor flaws should all be recorded in the inspector's report. Stained carpets and malfunctioning heating or cooling units should not be deciding factors in rejecting a property. Large repairs, however, such as plumbing damage, water damage, or leaky roofs should be handled with caution. While you should not be unrealistic in your expectations, it is worth trying to negotiate repair costs into your purchase offer. The owners may be willing to make repairs themselves, or may settle for a lower price if damages are significant.

Make Sure You Can Afford the House You Want

It is not uncommon for buyers to overlook financial costs and end up in a difficult financial position after purchasing a home that is outside of their price range. There are many financial factors that must be considered prior to buying a home. Because of this, it is important to take into account every debt, bill, or fee, including those that you will incur with loan and mortgage payments after making a purchase.

Can you truly afford your dream property, or will purchasing it turn your dream into a nightmare? The first financial items you will want to consider are those you will incur after purchasing your home. Consider the cost of your down payment. Most lenders require 10-20% of the total cost as a down payment. Consider your loan amount, as well as your loan period. Consider the closing costs. Closing costs can be paid out of pocket, as part of your down payment, or added to your total loan amount.

Once you have figured out the above information, you should carefully examine the rest of your financial situation. Let's take a look at some financial considerations you cannot afford to ignore.

Can You Afford Your Living Expenses?

You must make sure you can afford not only your loan repayment fees, but also your current and projected living expenses. Be sure to add up the following expenses:

- Utilities

- Car payments

- Car insurance

- Health insurance

- Weekly groceries

- Other debts or bills

Be sure to plan for the worst, as well. What will happen if you fall into financial hardship? Make sure you can really afford your new home and the payments that come along with it. Just because a lender qualifies you for a loan does not mean you can afford it. Be careful not to get in over your head – a major mistake many home buyers make. Do not forget to add up your home costs as well. Home costs you must take into consideration include the following:

- Lawyer fees

- Home inspection fees

- Extermination fees, if needed

- Escrow fees

You will also want to consider what the home needs and how it applies to your financial situation. Will you be able to afford necessary repairs before you move into your new home? Keep in mind that there will be other expenses once you move into your new home. New home expenses include:

- Desired renovations

- Decorating costs

- Furniture and other items

- General maintenance and upkeep

- Home owner's insurance

- Security system, if desired

Finally, be sure you take the time to plan for the future. Your future will greatly affect your current financial situation and financial strength. Do you have a family, or plan on starting one soon? Are you planning on getting married, taking a trip, or making a career change? These things, if the expense is too great, can make your mortgage payments more burdensome than they should be.

It should be clear to you by now that buying a home is not as simple as choosing a house and moving in. It is a complicated and often drawn out process. The cost of buying a house goes far beyond its initial price tag. Every cost and expense that comes along with purchasing a home should be weighed and considered before you make a decision. When you finally feel ready to make an offer, you should consult a financial advisor, who can direct you in how much of a loan you will need, as well as helping you determine what you can really afford in terms of payments. A good financial advisor will examine your entire budget and help you select a financing plan that is right for you, which can prevent you from getting into a financial bind later on.

Multiple Listing Service

The Multiple Listing Service, also known as MLS, is a convenient database used by realtors and brokers that shows every property currently on the market. Properties are added to the MLS database as soon they are available, and are removed as soon as they are not. The MLS does not cost any money to use, as it is a free service available to realtors and used to advertise their listings.

The MLS offers more options to the buyer, due to the high volume of properties that are listed. Because the MLS also lists property details, the buyer is able to discover and view many properties from the comfort of their own home. Buyers who are able to use the Multiple Listing Service benefit greatly from the vast quantity of properties available to look through.

The Multiple Listing Service can be a useful tool for potential buyers in a number of ways. In addition to offering buyers more options and providing images of many properties, the MLS also makes it possible for the potential buyer to narrow down search results by preference. Information that can be used to narrow down the search includes such specifications as property size, location, and age. The buyer is then able to view a set of properties that fit their requirements, rather than searching through hundreds or thousands of listings, only to find unsuitable houses.

Finally, the Multiple Listing Service makes it possible for the prospective buyer to contact the realtor directly. The realtor's information is listed along with the information of the house, so that the buyer is able to speak with the realtor regarding the property. This cuts out much of the stressful searching involved in finding and buying a home.

The MLS has been a huge asset to prospective home buyers everywhere. The database makes it easier to find desirable properties, and easier than ever to contact a realtor about their listing. The MLS is both convenient and safe to use, making it the ultimate tool for people looking to purchase a home. More real estate choices mean it is easier to make a better decision regarding a property purchase. This alone makes the MLS invaluable to home buyers.

How to Hire a Good Real Estate Agent

A good real estate agent is a huge part of your home buying experience, and is ultimately crucial to the success of your endeavour. While buying a house can be a thrilling and exciting experience, it can also be very stressful and, at times, unpleasant. An effective real estate agent is able to minimize your stress about buying a home, making the entire process more enjoyable. Let's look at what you need to know to find and keep a good real estate agent.

Know Your Agent

Knowing who you are hiring for the job is crucial to both your success and the agent's. Be sure to verify the agent's license as well as their state real estate license for property sales. This will keep you from getting scammed by an unlicensed agent. It is also a good idea to do a brief background check on your potential real estate agent. This can include asking about previous properties the agent has successfully bought or sold for clients. It does not hurt to get an idea of what kind of education, training, and seminars the agent has experienced, either.

Build a Relationship

It is beneficial to both yourself and the agent to choose an agent that you have some chemistry with. You will want to try to build a strong professional relationship soon after meeting your agent. You can encourage the development of a strong professional relationship by telling your agent exactly what you are looking for in a house, your budget, and any other relevant details. The agent should, in turn, be completely honest with you about worth and value of a property. Also, be sure to meet up with your agent occasionally to discuss properties and any questions you may have outside of the usual paperwork. This will build a strong relationship between yourself and the agent which can help ensure that your agent is on your side.

Your Agent and Your Purchase

An agent is a crucial part of the home buying process. Your agent will be your researcher in finding available properties and discovering important facts like average market value in your desired neighborhood. The agent is also responsible for acting as a go-between for yourself and the property seller; they are charged with offering you advice about desirable vs. undesirable properties, suggested offers, and more. Your agent should be very knowledgeable on all of these subjects.

If you are going to hire an agent, be sure you hire a good one. Check out their credentials, education, training, and their history in the field. Your agent is a key part of helping you, as the buyer, to determine whether or not you are getting a good deal. Because of this, if you are careful in your agent selection, you will almost definitely have a pleasant purchasing experience.

Hanging on to Your Money

Buying property is quite expensive, in some cases overwhelmingly so. It is very easy to go broke after buying a house. Even if you do not put down a large down payment, minimizing your out of pocket expense, signing a mortgage is still a huge financial responsibility that puts you deep into debt. In short, buying a home is a huge financial commitment.

There are a variety of other expenses included with buying which are excluded from the initial purchase and related fees. Moving expenses, storage expenses, and potential tax consequences add up to a high bill with the potential to last a lifetime.

You worked hard to find a great deal on your prospecting home, and negotiated the lowest price possible. One way or another, you have to pay the mortgage, the down payment, the closing costs, and sometimes agent fees. Your closing costs include many expensive items, such as home insurance, title expenses, and much more. Don't want to hand out more cash? I don't blame you! Let's see some tips that can help you save your money.

Have Good Credit and Financing

Before you start house hunting, make sure your credit is in order. Good credit will reduce your interest rates and improve your financing options. Once your credit is in order, secure favorable financing. Shop around from banks, lenders and mortgage companies to find the lowest interest rates available for your credit score. Negotiate your fees firmly, and, unless your credit is very poor and you have no other options, try to avoid paying a large loan application fee. This will put more money in your pocket and less money in your creditors'.

Repeat the shopping around process with everyone involved. Be sure to watch out for title companies, who are known for having high fees. A rush delivery fee of $50 or more to deliver your paperwork is not uncommon. Do not give any creditors, lenders, or title companies free rein with your money. You have the right to say how much they can and cannot spend. Keep in mind that you are not required to choose the title company your agent recommends, as they may have higher fees. Feel free to shop around and find a lower rated title company if possible. This is a great way to save money, but one that many people overlook.

Your title company and your lender will recommend an insurance company to you as well. There is a good chance that both companies will attempt to bully you into using the company they recommend because it will create less paperwork for them. Remember that you are in control of your own finances, and you do not have to choose a company just because it was recommended to you. Often, you can find lower rated insurance through a company that your lender and title company did not recommend. Do not be afraid to shop around!

Be sure to ask your lender what financing options are available for your individual credit score. It is possible to find loans that require low down payments. Some loans require down payments as low as 5%, while others require no down payment. However, if you select one of these financing plans, be cautious and read the fine print. They are often accompanied by higher than average interest rates.

Do not be hasty in selecting a financing plan. Slow down and take the time you need to shop around effectively. Keep in mind that there are financing options available that cause the seller to pay a higher percentage of the closing costs. Occasionally, the seller will pay all of the closing costs. However, be aware that avoiding the closing costs usually means the amount is combined to your loan amount.

While the last few years have been a seller's market, in which the seller has advantages over the buyer, things are changing again. Even if you are looking to buy a property during a seller's market, it does not mean that the seller will necessarily be rigid in their demands. Some situations, such as having a fixed move out date or a strong need for money, can cause the seller to bend to the buyer's demands. Again, shopping around is the best way to get a great house for the lowest price possible.

It is your money. Do not let anyone rush you into a financial decision; give yourself the time to shop around for the best deal you can find. This will ultimately keep more money in your pocket.

How to Spot a Scam Before It Spots You

Unfortunately, scams exist in the real estate market as much as anywhere else. Most people want to buy their own home, and the fastest and often easiest way to do so is by applying for a home loan through a mortgage company. Mortgage loaning is a huge business, and with the amount of mortgage companies trying to lure you in, you have to know how to spot a scam.

There are crooked mortgage companies who will try to scam you out of your money. It is no concern of theirs if you lose your savings, your house, or if you are forced to file bankruptcy. These crooked companies do not care about you or your finances; they are only looking out for themselves. They are not concerned with your well-being or financial security, but are instead concerned with lining their pockets. First time home buyers are easy prey for mortgage company scams, and it is easy to fall into their trap once they have made their seductive deals and propositioned you.

It should be clear that mortgage scams are very real and very dangerous for your financial security. Let's look at some tips that will expose a mortgage scam or crooked company. Following these tips will help keep you out of their clutches.

1. Beware of Vague Information

Beware if your mortgage company is unable or unwilling to give you an estimate of the closing costs on your property. According to the Real Estates Settlement Act, this information must be provided to buyers within three days of your loan application being submitted. An honest mortgage company has nothing to hide and will not have any problem supplying you with this information, often before you have even requested it. An excellent mortgage company is even capable of providing you with an estimate on your closing costs based only on your pre-qualifying information. The bottom line is, a company who will not give you information regarding costs and fees up front is not a company you want to sign paperwork with.

2. Beware of Lies

Beware if your mortgage company tells you it is okay to falsify your financial information. Mortgage scams often involve counseling a buyer to falsify their financial information in order to increase their chances of loan approval. This should be a red flag for you. Lying on a loan application, no matter how insignificant, is a criminal act and is considered fraud. While it may increase your chances of approval, the long term consequences are not worth the risk. Use common sense when dealing with a mortgage company. Any company who encourages you to commit fraud will have no problem committing fraud with your loan information.

3. Beware Too Good to be True Offers

Beware if your mortgage company makes an offer that is too good to be true. A common way to hook unwitting buyers into a mortgage scam is to offer them interest rates that are 2-3% lower than everyone else. Both very low interest rates and very high interest rates should be a warning sign of a fraudulent mortgage company. It might seem like an incredibly low interest rate on your mortgage is a good way to save some money, but, in the long run, it will actually cost you much more. This is because extremely low interest rates are rarely fixed, which will lead to your rates increasing astronomically over the years.

People with undesirably low credit scores are prone to falling victim to high interest rate scams. These people often feel that they have no other choice but to accept the high interest rate. These interest rates may only be 2-3% higher than every other mortgage company, but that is enough to point out a possible scam. There are websites available in which a potential buyer can get an interest rate estimate based entirely on their credit score. This will give you a better idea of what you should be paying versus what certain companies want you to pay.

4. Beware of Pressure

Beware if you are pressured into accepting an offer from any mortgage company, especially if you feel that you do not understand the terms or are financially incapable of making the required payments. A common ploy of fraudulent mortgage companies is to tell low-credit buyers that they will be unable to find a loan through any other company. You should remember that a good mortgage company will never pressure you into signing anything. A good mortgage company will also take the time to explain terms and conditions, and will not try to sign you up for a loan you definitely cannot afford. If you ask for clarification and are still confused, it may be helpful to speak to a real estate lawyer, who can discuss the loan in detail with you. Remember that if one company is offering you a loan, another company will as well. You are never limited to one option, and should never feel pressured to sign anything.

Read your contract carefully prior to signing a mortgage with any mortgage company. Be very careful to make sure that the contract you sign is exactly the same as the contract you agreed to. You will also want to be cautious of companies who request additional signers, credit insurance, or any prepayment fees, as these companies are generally attempting to make money off of your loan agreement.

The bottom line is, if a company feels like it does not have your best interests in mind, it probably does not. Be cautious when proceeding with these companies. If you feel pressured or uncomfortable in any way, seek a loan with a different mortgage company. There are plenty of companies available who are willing to offer you a loan and to work with you, while keeping your best interests in mind. Let's look at ways to avoid being trapped financially in a mortgage scam by a fraudulent company.

Creative Ways to Finance Your Home

For quite some time, 80/20 has been the standard financing option. 80/20 financing means 80% of your property's cost comes out of a loan, while 20% is provided by your down payment. 20% of a property's cost can be quite a large sum of money, which makes it fortunate for you that the times have changed significantly.

There are now a vast variety of financing options available to help you secure your home. A popular option is to take out a second mortgage through a different bank or lender than the original home loan. This allows the buyer to put in 5% of the down payment themselves, while borrowing the remaining 15% from another lender. While this may seem like a good option, there are also repercussions. Not only does the buyer have to worry about the second mortgage's high interest rate, but private mortgage insurance is usually also required.

Private mortgage insurance, or PMI, often involves hefty fees for the buyer which may not make the most sense financially. It is, however, theoretically possible for the lender to remove the PMI. This usually occurs after a significant amount of on-time loan payments have been made, but does not happen often. Most often, the buyer ends up re-financing the loan or selling the property before the PMI is removed.

For the ambitious buyer, there are other financing options available. For example, a buyer who is quick to snatch up a property in a new housing development may be pleased to find that the developers are willing to fund a home loan. This is not always the case, but if you are able to get an offer in on a new property quick enough, you may be lucky enough to find a manufacturer's loan at only 5% of the property's purchase price.

Daring buyers with excellent credit have other options available as well. If your credit is good enough, you may be able to buy a house without putting your name on the title, and immediately sell the established contract from somewhere between $500 and $5,000. While this option is risky, it allows home owners to turn a small but quick profit on the property.

Yet another form of creative financing is the sub-2 deal. A sub-2 deal occurs when the seller deeds their home to the buyer, but keeps the home's original mortgage in place. While the mortgage loan is never legally in your name, you simply start making payments as though it were. This is an arrangement that can be beneficial for both the buyer and the seller, but is not recommended for the beginner.

Creative buyers can also utilize a limited partnership, in which the details can greatly vary. In some cases, each partner will assume 50% of the property's financial responsibility. In other cases, one person assumes the financial responsibility while the other person is responsible for maintenance, repairs, and upkeep. These deals are extremely versatile, and can be mutually beneficial for both partners.

Government loans are also available to people who fit a specific set of circumstances. Some government loans include military loans and low income loans. These loans are almost always limited to the people who intend to occupy the property, so getting a loan in someone else's name is not an option.

Credit cards are also an available financing option, though this is not highly recommended. This option comes with a much higher interest rate than you would expect to find through a mortgage company. Additionally, credit card companies examine any and all outstanding debt when making a decision, rather than just looking at your credit score. With this method, something as simple as a cash advance can get you quickly denied for a loan.

Finally, you can accept a loan or gift from friends and family. However, most mortgage companies view this as a debt unless you can prove without a doubt that the money was a gift rather than a loan. Mortgage companies cannot be tricked. They have seen every trick in the book already, so avoid trying to fool them – it usually does not end well for the buyer.

FICO: Your Credit Score and You

Understanding your credit score is an important part of the mortgage loan process. It is close to impossible to take out a home loan or even find out information on a home loan if you do not know your credit score. Credit scores are available through a variety of websites or over the phone, but it is not as simple as knowing the number.

Most buyers figure out early on in the loan process just how important their credit score is. Your credit score will determine your approval for a loan, and will also weigh heavily on your loan's interest rate.

Your credit score is determined by your credit history. A record of all of your credit history is logged into a computer system and analyzed in order to provide you with your personal credit rating, or credit score. Credit scores are sometimes called FICO scores. This is because most of the software used in calculating your credit score was developed by Fair Isaac Corporation.

There are things you need to know to understand your credit score and what it means for you. Most importantly, you will want to know how your credit score is calculated. Let's take a look.

Past Payment Records

Your past payment records make up 35% of your credit score. Lending companies are able to see every late payment, your amount past due, and the amount of time it has been since you have made a late payment. The more on track your payment history is, the higher your credit score will be.

Debt Amounts

Your debt amounts account for 30% of your credit score. Lending companies are able to see how many lines of credit you have, how many different companies you have credit with, and how many times, if any, you have been over your credit limit.

Credit History

The length of your credit history makes up 15% of your credit score. The length of your credit history refers to how long you have had accounts open, as well as how often your accounts are in use. The longer your credit history is, the better your credit score is.

Credit Type

The types of credit you have make up 10% of your credit score. There are many types of credit. A variety of credit types present on your credit history, rather than just credit card accounts, will increase your overall credit score.

New Credit

Your new credit accounts make up the remaining 10% of your credit score. Lending companies are able to see how many credit applications you have made, as well as how many new accounts you have open. Opening too many new accounts or getting rejected on several credit applications in a short period of time will lower your credit score.

So, What Makes A Good Credit Score?

Are you wondering what makes a good credit score versus a bad one? For starters, credit scores typically range somewhere between 350 and 850. The higher your score is, the better your credit is. Conversely, the lower your score is, the worse your credit is. Individuals with high credit scores are considered a low financial risk, and are often eligible for home loans at low interest rates.

It is never too late to improve your credit score. While it takes time, it can certainly be done. You can start by making sure you pay your bills on time and keep a low balance on your credit cards. It also helps to make a few dollars more than the minimum payment on all of your accounts each month. Try to avoid opening several credit accounts at once, as this can also negatively impact your credit score.

Lenders are more likely to give a loan to a person who can prove their financial responsibility, and this is exactly what your credit score does. You will want to get a detailed credit report and make sure that your report is up to date and accurate, as mistakes or out of date reports can negatively impact your credit score. Remember that the amount of debt you have is not the only thing that impacts your FICO score. How you manage your debt is equally important; it can improve or damage your credit rating, so be careful!

Loan Pre-Approval and What It Means

Have you been pre-approved for a home loan? This is excellent, as it gives you an advantage over other home buyers. Competitive buyers who are not financially secure and are not pre-approved may have a harder time securing a home loan than someone who is already pre-approved. Taking the steps to get loan pre-approval shows the seller of the property that you are serious about buying, and this looks good for you. Let's take a look at how to become pre-approved for a home loan.

How to Get Pre-Approved

Evaluate your current financial situation honestly. This is a good place to start when seeking loan pre-approval. Draw up two lists. The first list should contain all of your assets. Assets include cash, bonds, savings, stock, and IRAs, as well as other things. The second list should contain all of your debts. Debts include car payments, loans, and credit card debt.

The difference between the two lists will give you a good idea of how much money you can allot towards buying a home. However, keep in mind that buying a home comes along with additional expenses, many of which we discussed earlier. The difference in the lists will also give you a pretty good idea of how much money you will be able to borrow in order to purchase a house. This information will help you get pre-approved for a loan.

Being pre-approved for a loan is essentially a simple process. Getting your pre-approval will put you one step ahead of competitive buyers, and will get you one step closer to signing paperwork for your new home. You should note that being pre-approved is different than being pre-qualified. Pre-qualification happens when you provide a lender with your credit report and are then qualified for a loan. This process is largely based on your reports and is not verified by paperwork, making your qualification as thin as the paper it is printed on. On the other hand, pre-approval is a commitment from a lender stating that they will give you a loan in the amount they determine based on your credit rating.

Loan pre-approval gives you quite an advantage when you are shopping for a home. Because you know your actual budget, it also allows you to seek out homes that are in your price range, rather than bidding for them later, only to be disappointed. This will give you an advantage over a buyer who is not pre-approved, since the seller will be more likely to make a quick decision based on your pre-approval status.

Getting pre-approved will help you choose a suitable home. It will also put you in a better position to negotiate price with the seller, which can save you money and speed up the buying process. You will want to make sure you get a pre-approval statement from your lender, as a pre-qualification letter is not enough to give you much of an advantage in the housing market. Once you are aware of your budget after being pre-approved, you can begin shopping around for a home with a price that fits your budget.

While your agent may encourage you to do so, it is unwise to allow your real estate agent to act as your mortgage loan officer. This can give you problems when securing a loan. Instead, you should get referrals from family, friends, neighbours, and colleagues. Speak to a couple of different loan officers, and try to secure an APR that is suitable for your financial situation.

Understanding Loan Options

There are many different loan options available to you. The vast variety of mortgage loan options can make it extremely difficult to select an option that is right for you and your financial needs. In order to find a loan that is suitable for you, let's take a look at the three major types of home loans.

1. Fixed Mortgage Loans

The fixed mortgage loans are the most popular type of home loan. There are several terms of fixed rate loans available.

30 Year Fixed Rate:

This loan term spreads your loan payments over 30 years. It is the most popular loan term. Advantages include lower monthly payments and less financial burden. Disadvantages include paying more on the loan in the long run. This is the best option for buyers who plan to stay in their home permanently.

15 Year Fixed Rate:

The 15 year fixed rate spreads your loan payments over 15 years. Advantages include paying half of the interest of a 30 year loan. Disadvantages include higher monthly payments and a larger financial burden.

Bi-weekly Loan:

The bi-weekly loan is paid every 2 weeks instead of once a month. While bi-weekly loans are usually thirty year terms, you actually end up paying off your loan in about 23 years. Advantages include repaying your loan faster, and less overall interest. Disadvantages include having to keep track of two monthly payments instead of one.

Adjustable Rate Mortgage (ARM):

Adjustable rate mortgages work directly off of interest rates which means your interest rate generally starts out lower than other fixed rate plans. While this means you start off paying lower interest rates, your rates are subject to increase. Advantages include your payment decreasing as your interest rate decreases. Disadvantages include your payments going up if your interest rate increases.

2. Convertible Loans

Convertible loans are not as popular as fixed rate loans. However, these loans are suitable for some home owners. Let's take a look at different types of convertible loans.

Hybrid/Convertible Adjustable Rate Mortgage Loan:

This loan option actually includes two types of loans: an adjustable rate mortgage which can be converted to a fixed rate loan, or a fixed rate loan that can be converted to an adjustable rate mortgage. This loan type offers flexibility to the home owner. Advantages include the ability to adjust your interest rates. Disadvantages include being subject to high interest rates, which can leave you unwilling to change your loan type.

Interest Only Loan:

This type of loan is suitable for home owners who do not have steady work, but are paid on commission or work in a career that offers somewhat regular bonuses. An interest only loan allows the buyer to pay only the interest on the loan, and make payments on the actual loan when they receive additional funds. This is the equivalent of paying off only the interest on a credit card, in that it holds your loan amount steady without either rising or falling. Advantages include the ability to receive a larger home loan. Disadvantages include making no progress on your loan amount when paying only the interest.

Balloon Loan:

This loan type is a fixed rate loan that requires the home owner to make modest monthly payments for approximately seven years. At the end of the first period, the home owner is required to either pay off the property in a lump sum or refinance the loan. Advantages include the ability to pay low interest rates if you want to sell your home prior to the entry period ending. Disadvantages include the necessity to come up with a large sum of money or refinance the loan at a potentially much higher interest rate.

Reverse Mortgage Loan:

Reverse mortgage loans are great for seniors, or people on a fixed income. These loans require no monthly payments, but the entire loan must be paid off once the house is sold. Advantages include more money in your pocket due to lack of repayment. Disadvantages include reduced equity and/or need for repayment if the house is sold.

Buy Down Loan:

Buy down loans come with two options: temporary or permanent. Buy down loans work on a points system, as well as working with lower interest rates. Advantages include lower interest rates and greater savings. Disadvantages include the need to supply a more substantial down payment.

3. Special Mortgage Loans

Special mortgage loans are available for buyers who fit certain requirements. There are two types of special mortgage loans.

FHA Mortgage:

The FHA mortgage is only available to first time home owners, people who are unable to make a large down payment, and people with poor credit. Advantages include a low down payment and reduced loan repayment rates. Disadvantages include a limit on the available loan amount.

Veteran Affairs Loan:

The veteran affairs loan is only available for past and present members of the military and their widows. Advantages include a lack of a required down payment. Disadvantages include a longer loan approval process.

Clearly, there are many options available for repaying your home loan. The best way to find out which loan option is right for you is to discuss your options with a financial advisor. Your advisor will recommend loan options that are right for you and your financial needs.

Finding the Perfect Mortgage

With the vast amount of mortgage options available to homeowners today, it is no wonder that the mortgage process is subject to so much confusion. Not only are there many types of loans available, but the number of companies giving out loans is overwhelming. Mortgage companies, lenders, banks, credit unions, credit card companies, and finance companies are just a few types of companies that offer home loans.

With the large amount of loan options available, it is no surprise that finding the perfect mortgage plan is not an easy task. Prior to even applying for the loan, it is helpful to have a knowledge of the different options available to you. This will help you navigate the loan process much easier and more effectively. If there is a single truth that dominates the real estate market, it is that you should never choose a loan plan based on interest rates alone. Instead, familiarize yourself with the terminology that will present itself in your loan descriptions. You may then wish to shop around for a better deal. Do not be afraid to ask around, look online, or discuss your options with other lenders. There is plenty of advertisement available today that should make finding a loan easy. Use it!

In order to decide which kind of loan will suit your financial and lifestyle needs, you should ask your mortgage lender a handful of questions. Let's take a look at questions you should ask your mortgage lender before deciding what loan option is right for you.

1. How Long is the Approval Process?

You can expect your loan application to take 45-60 days to be approved. However, things occasionally happen faster, and your loan could theoretically be approved in as little as 60 days. The length of your approval process is dependent on your lender's speed with submitting paperwork.

2. What Documents Do You Need?

Your lender will need you to provide copies of a variety of documents. You will need to provide proof of income and proof of assets, but beyond that lenders vary in their required paperwork.

3. What Do I Need To Qualify?

Different lenders have different home loan qualifications. Your lender will definitely want to look at your financial information as well as your credit history and past buying experience, if any.

4. What Will My Minimum Down Payment Be?

Your down payment will determine your interest rates and terms of loans. Some loans may require 20% of the cost as your down payment while others are lower.

5. What Is My Annual Interest Rate?

It is important to know how much interest you will be paying annually. A good way to compare lenders' rates is to determine their annual percentage rate, or APR.

6. How Much are Origination Fees?

Origination fees are interest fees on your entire home loan. These fees are usually paid as prepaid mortgage interest. If you pay these fees at closing time, you can get a reduction in your overall interest rate.

7. Can I Lock in My Interest Rates?

Home loan interest rates fluctuate. Because of this, it is a smart move to lock in your interest rate for a set period of time. Be sure to ask your lender if there are fees involved for locking in your interest rate.

8. What is Your Estimate on Closing Costs?

Home mortgage loans are accompanied by a variety of fees. Ask for the entire mock-up of closing cost fees prior to signing.

9. Is There a Prepayment Penalty on the Loan?

Be sure to ask your lender to disclose the duration of the penalty period. You will also want to know the prepayment penalty rate.

Read the Fine Print

The most important precaution you can take prior to signing your loan papers is to read the fine print. Not reading your mortgage papers thoroughly could lead to a greater headache than it is worth. Keep in mind that your mortgage is a legally binding agreement, so you need to be aware of what you are signing.

Be sure to read every word of the fine print of your mortgage papers. It is okay to take as much time as necessary to go over this paperwork. It is better to take a little longer to complete your paperwork than it is to sign something you do not fully agree with, or, worse yet, that you do not understand. Reading your mortgage papers carefully can save you a good deal of time and money in the long run. Let's take a look at some of the things to watch out for while reviewing your loan papers.

Balloon Payment:

If you have not selected a balloon loan, watch out for mention of a balloon payment in the fine print. Some lenders will include this in the fine print, when it is not what you think you are agreeing to. Many buyers are happy to see that their repayment rates will be lower than expected, but are ultimately displeased to realize what a balloon payment entails. Be sure to check for these terms in the fine print, and read it carefully.

Notes:

Familiarize yourself with the terminology that is listed in the note section of your fine print. The note section may include conditions such as, if your loan payments are late, the lender reserves the right to seize and sell your property. The note may also mention that you will be liable for any additional fees, as well as the lenders' right to seize your assets if you fail to make regular payments.

Notice:

The notice portion of your mortgage papers' fine print is one of the most crucial sections for you to read cautiously. This section states how much notice, if any, the lender will provide if you fail to make your payments. Some lenders give no notice prior to seizing your home and assets, so make sure you send in your payments even if you are out of town. It is smart to send your mortgage payment early so you know it has been received prior to the deadline, or, if possible, send your payments electronically to cut down on transit and processing time. This will ensure that your mortgage payments arrive on time and will keep you from losing your home and your assets.

Acceleration:

The acceleration clause of your fine print section is also important. This section will state whether or not the lender reserves the right to speed up your repayment, and may also state that the lender is allowed to demand the entire loan repayment as a lump sum, should you miss a payment.

Additional Fees:

When you are going over your mortgage papers, be sure to recall agreed upon fees. You will want to watch out for any undisclosed or unexpected fees that may be listed in the fine print.

When you are reviewing your mortgage papers, it is important to make sure that every detail of the loan and its repayment is exactly what you agreed upon. Reading your paperwork carefully can save you the hassle of being presented with unexpected fees, terms, and conditions.

Reading and understanding your mortgage paperwork is a huge task, and not easily accomplished. It is very important that you know exactly what you are agreeing to before you sign your papers. Do not let anyone rush the process along. Take all the time you need to thoroughly understand your papers, especially the fine print. If at any point you become confused, remember that it is your right to have the paperwork explained to you. Do not sign anything you do not fully understand. You may also choose to have someone else examine your mortgage papers. If there is any time during the buying process that a lawyer is an asset, it is during the signing phase. If you feel the need, have your lawyer go over the fine print and explain things, or point out any conditions you may have missed.

Insurance and Risk Management: Everything You Need to Know

First, let's take a look at some real estate statistics. In 2005, the average residential property price rose by 15% from the previous year. During this time, lenders lowered typical credit score requirements, raised the standard debt allowance up to 45% of yearly income, and waived certain documentation requirements. Since then, reports have suggested that an estimated 30% of new home loans are interest-only loans, which were previously uncommon. On top of that, another 35% of mortgages are adjustable rate mortgages, and the U.S. Federal Reserve has raised interest rates a total of 11 times.

What do these numbers mean for new home buyers? They mean, in a nutshell, that the real estate market has seen major growth since 2005. Unfortunately, rapid price increases, both on homes and interest rates, always mean increases in risks. Fortunately for the new home buyer, there is currently an insurance plan to cover just about any risk you may feel the need to take. The most common forms of insurance that benefit the buyer are title insurance and liability insurance. Let's take a look at these types of insurance.

Title Insurance

Title insurance is designed to cover any financial lapses that may have occurred prior to closing taking place. Title insurance covers any potential financial loss that may occur as the result of errors with the title process.

Errors with the title process occur because, while title companies search public records to make sure a title is clear, people make mistakes. It is easy for a title company to miss a public record, or for the record to be omitted from databases. This could result in a tax lien against the property. Title insurance will cover your losses due to potential errors up to a specified monetary limit.

Liability Insurance

Liability insurance is designed to cover any injuries that may occur on the property. Any time someone is on your property and sustains an injury, liability insurance will cover expenses like medical bills and the settlement of any lawsuits, up to a specified monetary limit.

There are additional forms of insurance available for just about any scenario or disaster you can imagine. Hazard insurance covers more than a dozen hazardous situations, including many natural disasters such as floods, fires, and tornadoes. Sometimes hazard insurance will also cover damages from things like wind or freezing temperatures. Some hazard insurance policies also cover man-made hazards, such as chemical spills, electrical failures, and unnatural accidental fires.

Insurance plans cover a vast array of risks including vandalism, burglary, faulty electrical systems, faulty plumbing, and malfunctioning appliances. Landlords are also eligible for additional policies, which cover the expenses in case a tenant is unable to pay their rent.

Of course, it is to be expected that every type of insurance comes at a price. Insurance plan prices vary depending on the plan type and the amount of damages covered. Insurance plans are also accompanied by a variety of conditions on which payment is not the responsibility of the insurance company. As with anything else, when it comes to buying a home do not be afraid to shop around for the best coverage and rates. This will save you money, but will also offer more protection for your property and everyone on it.

Despite the many types of insurance plans to choose from, you are required to get one insurance plan, and have no say in the matter. If you take out a mortgage loan, you are required to purchase mortgage insurance which pays the lender in the event of your failure to make your payments.

Save Money With an Inspection

Real estate comes in a large variety of conditions. The best way to know if a desired property is a sound investment is to have it professionally inspected. When you are making a deal with a seller, you should include in writing that any deal agreed upon is dependent upon a satisfactory inspection. Next, let's take a look at what constitutes a satisfactory inspection.

Freedom from Pests

Unless you are moving into a woodless brick home, you will want to get a separate inspection for pest or termite damage. The majority of home inspectors will not check for termite damage, so it is up to you to find someone who will. Spotting a termite problem could save you thousands of dollars down the road. Pests, in general, can cause huge financial repercussions for a property, so you will want to make sure the house is vermin free. If it is not, you can sometimes negotiate with the seller and get them to cover extermination costs prior to your move in date.

No Structural Damage

Your home inspector will carefully examine the structures of the property, beginning with the foundation. The foundation will be checked for large cracks, uneven ground, and water damage or leaking. The inspector will go over every part of the house's structure carefully, including the floors, walls, ceilings, and much more. The inspector will look for improper material use, poor maintenance, or structural damage.

The inspector will also examine the house's plumbing and electrical. The inspector is responsible for making sure that the plumbing and electrical systems are up to code and in good shape. Leaks will be noted, and the pipes will be carefully examined for rust, lead, or chemical build up. During the electrical system review, the inspector will seek out faulty wiring, improper grounding, inadequate circuit breakers, and more. All of this will be done to ensure that the plumbing and electrical systems are completely up to code.

The inspector will work his way up to the attic, where he will check for proper framing, structural strength, and will examine the general air quality. The underside of the roof is also examined from the attic. The inspector will also examine the roof from the outside, looking for any leaks or damage.

The inspector is also responsible for checking the exterior of the house by looking for leaky faucets and pipes. Inside the house, the inspector will check appliances such as any heating and cooling units. Any built in appliances that may be present will also be checked for wear and tear and proper functioning. Finally, the inspector will go over surface details such as carpet condition and the presence of any mold or water damage.

There is much more to an inspector's job. Basically, they inspect the entire house, inside and out, from top to bottom. All of the inspector's findings are noted in a detailed report, which is then provided to the buyer. The buyer can then use defective items in the home as negotiation points for lowering a seller's asking price or requesting that repairs be made prior to the sale's completion. An inspection is also beneficial to the seller, who may choose to make necessary repairs prior to putting the house on the real estate market.

For both parties, the inspection is a key step to the buying process that costs a few hundred dollars but can save thousands in the long run. An inspection allows the buyer to know exactly what they are buying, and allows the seller to know what changes should be made to get the most money for their property sale.

Preparing to Buy a Home

Throughout this manual, you should have learned all you need to know about buying your first home. Keep in mind that you have rights. You should know these rights, and should not be afraid to stand up for them. Also, do not be afraid to shop around for the best deals and ask any questions you may have. Gather up all of your information prior to seeking and buying a home. Be sure to review this information before you sign any paperwork.

Most of all, remember that in the real estate game, knowledge is not just power it is priceless.

We Want Your Feedback on This Book!

Our main purpose is to make sure that our readers get value from the books we publish and that they have a good experience with all of our products. We are always working to improve our books and other products with every revision and update.

Every piece of feedback makes a difference in this process. And we would appreciate yours as well - whether it is good or bad.

Please take one minute to let us know what you thought by following this link:
http://checkmatemg.com/feedbackhomebuying

www.ingramcontent.com/pod-product-compliance
Lightning Source LLC
Chambersburg PA
CBHW071817170526
45167CB00003B/1336